# Flowing Words

Thornrose

 pencil

ISBN 978-93-5667-133-1
© Thornrose 2022
Published in India 2022 by Pencil

*A brand of*
One Point Six Technologies Pvt. Ltd.
123, Building J2, Shram Seva Premises,
Wadala Truck Terminal, Wadala (E)
Mumbai 400037, Maharashtra, INDIA
**E** connect@thepencilapp.com
**W** www.thepencilapp.com

*All rights reserved worldwide*

No part of this publication may be reproduced, stored in or introduced into a retrieval system, or transmitted, in any form, or by any means (electronic, mechanical, photocopying, recording or otherwise), without the prior written permission of the Publisher. Any person who commits an unauthorized act in relation to this publication can be liable to criminal prosecution and civil claims for damages.

DISCLAIMER: *The opinions expressed in this book are those of the authors and do not purport to reflect the views of the Publisher.*

# Author biography

A SIMPLE WOMAN WITH AN OVER EMOTIONAL HEART AND OVERTHOUGHTFUL MIND.
LAUGHS IN RAIN , SLEEPS IN DREAMS AND WRITES IN LOVE.

# CONTENTS

# Acknowledgements


TO MY CRAZY DYSFUNCTIONAL FAMILY ......LOVE FOREVER.

# ATHEIST

I don't bend and fold my hands
And settle down on my knees to pray
They call me an Atheist
This is twisted identification they say.
My morality is what I pride on
The life teaching the lessons of karma
The blocks of prayers aren't inviting
The structure of my conscience is
Divinity is an ascension of soul

# BLOCK

"Don't pull the trigger"
The prompt screams.
The mind blanks out
The writer shivers
The words feel hot
The punctuation paralyzes
And
the space is relieved.

# BOOK-AFFAIR

We meet
Your smell and touch makes me thrilled
I want to know you
Pages unfold
And love happens
The enormous laughters, a lump in the throat
My senses yielding to words you say
Time loses sleep over the love which stays
The exhilarating intimacy
You put to end
When you go back being 'The Book I read'.

# CLOSURE

Does something like Closure exists?
Does its definition match with anything in real life?
Turn me into that direction.
Because I m not still sure.
Is it on moments we blended together
Or is it on memories we have melded forever.
The bridges are to be burnt
Or gaps to be stretched.
Do we get our time back
Or we use the time machine?
The heart needs answers
The brain seems scraped
Closure is under construction.

# DEFINITE

Today I came across this sudden burst of timid yellow
Strong power it had
It made my abode little more mellow
Mellow??
Yes ..it did
The tint of colour lifted the red
Red which rolled as fury and melancholy
Bit of this hue
Hinting at the pragmatic trace
We…yes we can do just like them
Perch on the branch of candor
Be the one….one worth for it.
Am happy I came across this burst of yellow.

# DOPPELGANGER

While walking down lanes of life
Hands swinging with the one I love
I crashed into my doppelganger and sprawled on the floor
It was my doppelganger
I never knew before.
"Weird you didn't see it coming"
Exclaimed the love
Weird, that's the connect of the resemblance.
Love laughed aloud as glad he was to fall for the unique one
Doppelganger smiled as the twisted traits complimented someone really straight.
Then the clock struck 12
Embellished visions engulfed us around
The only doppelganger to find was no where to be found.
We have started walking again the lanes
My head high this time
The idea is look straight in the eyes and not sprawl on floor again.
Doppelganger I am on my way.

# DREAMERS

Dreamers can't be tamed
They smile from corners of the sky blue
And sleep on the roars of rendezvous
Dreamers can't be tamed
What they wonder always matters
And what matters is always to be wondered .
Dreamers can't be tamed
Their canvas gets painted in colours of hue
Strokes and patterns all askew
Dreamers can't be tamed
The world is an acceptance of what it seems
Soul baring eyes is the mirror of all you see.

# DRY MOON

Who has hung the moon to dry?
The monsoon has just touched its rim
And drizzling showers had just begun.
The patched surface was soaking the drops
The luminous haze shined bright and light
The stars across went green with grim
The constellations conspired
They blew the grey ones away

# DRY WAVES

The wave lies low
Trail of residues along
The thalassophile walks slow
There is so much to prolong
High tide bought ectasy
Submerged all senses
How it feel so pure
Lived under pretences
The receding water fades
Disowns the passion
Bubbles get squashed
Thalassophile left soaked
Drenched footprints vanshing
Trudging thristy nearby
Sea rolled back
Mirage intensify
Water around
Ocean gets dry

# DUSK

Dusk is golden
Mystic on the horizons
Brings out the beauty of dark
And dreams begin to brighten
Skyline turns in blushing hues
Stars peep from their blanket
Evening becomes aglow
Embraces are in tow.

# EMOTIONS

I think I overthink
And then I feel more love
It fills my headt and flows to mind
Then I definitely overlove.
Ths seeds of emotions gets food
And the roots extend in whimsical ways
They take its course
Weakest and strongest, happiest and saddest
Build me up day by day
The everlasting effervescences
Makes me what I m today.

# ASHES

Exhausted mind refuses to believe
The unknown fear will have to wait
The combat lies weak
The ignition sparks gasp for flair
The steps of solidity crawls today
Life in stillness makes its way
It shall rise like a phoneix
Robust as fresh
As tomorrow will be a newfound day !!!

# FIND ME

And where can you find me…
In the morning quietness
Crisp headlines with adarak tea.
Hear me in the tinkling sound of the jhumkaa
Whispering sweet nottings  to the hair behind
Realize me in the music on the way
The rhythm and tunes will sing of me along
In the glance outside the evening window
See my sight in the radiating sky
Bavarian icecream will shout of my name
As will my books flip for same.
Hear me in words which parents speak
I am in laugh of conversations heaps
Pause to see there I am
In smiles and grins of Him
Sum of these are what form me
Discover me in these synonyms.

# PAST MIDNIGHT

Awake past midnight
Do thoughts race hard?
Awake past midnight
Does stress pulls apart?
Awake past midnight
Is it insomnia?
Awake past midnight
Must be vivacious imagination
Awake past midnight
Are silences soothing ?
Awake past midnight
Are words flowing …..

# PERCEPTION

Align and register
Tilt the over looming projection again
What is perched on the ledge
Is the view of your perception
Panoptic balance with consumed minds
What we conceive is what we find
The overcast of introspections
Leaves the scars of distorted vision
In the world of huge emotions
The space of choices of notions
The interlocking of the perfections
The jigsaw puzzle completes the connection.

# PERPLEXED

Perplexed I stand looking at the waves
The tides are turning and churning
The Moon is in full bloom
Stretching the heart
Asking to compromise
Passion and fury roll up and down
Standing astride I find myself entangled
The desire to be free and overwhelming lustre
The water soothes and scars
Leaving its traces like the dots on the moon
Soon this circle will be over
Tides will sleep and moon will hug
Perplexed me will be left drenched
Afterall it was my heart which was tugged.

# RAINS

The crazy skies
The roaring sensations
Its hard to comprehend who is more thirsty
The rising winds
The thundering downpour
Its hard to comprehend
What is more euphoric
The raving Gulzar
The adrak chai
Its hard to comprehend what is more pure
The rising spirit
The awakened desires
Its hard to comprehend
What is simple- life or love.

# CHILDHOOD

If I could re-live your childhood
What different would I do?
Will this silver maturity help?
Or that exploring experience was good.
Will I be able to build better pathways?
Or my building blocks of those times suffice.
In this new streaks of knowledge
Will techniques of those time have a price?
All my mistakes can they be erased?
Or do those errors play role in your make
I think, rethink, build and rebuild
What is it that my heart is looking for
Oh its your smiles, love and Johnson's fragrance
that your childhood has to be re-lieved for

# ROOM 509

I asked for my home
And end of corridor a flat kind was shown.
It was on 5th floor, view splendid and picturesque.
With some dithering I entered inside
Royally furnished it was a decor magazine alive. Alas here
my middle class stuff cant survive.
Your highness will be the title bestowed
On one ring wish people will show
The laptop and attire found its places
And the family sunk into comfortable spaces
Lazy breakfasts vibrant conversations and smiles plenty
The life took a tangent curve gently
Friends became family and moments got archived
Years five but seeemd a lifetime
The hotel my home bought us humbling experience
Yes we were the royalty who were blessed in time.

# ROTTEN POTATOES

The sack of rotten potatoes get heavy
Don't carry them along
Its not only the pungence
They unsettle you along
Shoulders create bonds
Benevolence makes heart glow
Wave back to laughing faces
Smile on the way back to the song
Perspectives build the character
Patterns add along
If they change your song
Then pause to check if the track is wrong

# MIDNIGHT RUMBLINGS

Roller-coaster ride some days it is
And then its deep silences roaring
When the stars play with the moonlight
The dreams in me keep snoring
Imagination rides high on glory
And intricate becomes the web of stories
The moon gets amused with the colliding reflections
The clock becomes the point of introspection
Life is as what it seems to be
The midnight musings bring calm to me.

# SCARS

Scars don't hurt.
They are a remembrance of the experience we had
For the trauma we recovered we are glad
They talk to mind of the moment and deed
The heart reminisces the point indeed
The soul is proud of the victory it had
The body radiates of the rejuvenation it got
Scars remain forever as eternal
To remind of wars we won internal

# SEASONS

In the crisp month November
The silver streaks meet
Play on the words
And sleep on the interlude
The tickles bring strides
And blooming grins just go wide
Portraits become mirrors
Longing for the voice
Desires are covertly deepeened
Ardor spreads in bloom
And then.......
Winter sets in.

# SOULS OF TRUTH

Are we ready to embrace beauty of truth?
It is in the souls around
Naked and wild, like beautiful smiles.
Lives of glamour quotient can't hold the mirror
Like a fresh dew drop truth shines through clear
Ambitions and desires wear the cloak
Heavy and zazzy of unspoken words
Shying away eyes close the doors of sincere urge
The luminous haze remains hidden
And souls getting tamed
Truth is dark… ugly, not to be claimed.
So are we ready to embrace beauty of truth

# STARRY CONVERSATIONS

Let's go to the terrace and I will show you my
conversations.
Conversations which every star has kept in heart
They tell a story each…of days and moments.
Moments which were unique and priceless.
Stars will make you blush and laugh
The stories so animated and robust
Stars twinkled and gleamed
While our chit-chats happened in flow
These stars will recite the dreams of mine
Ones with silver flowers on side
Listen to their whispers of minutes
My conversations are noted with smiling marks
Tip-toe quietly as my stars are naughty
My conversations with them are all illumanati.

# STRANGERS AGAIN

Being strangers were better
So much familiarity
And no place for being close
Being strangers were better
So much of familiarity
And no more secrets to disclose
Being strangers were better
So much of familiarity
And no comfort to show
Being strangers were better
So much of familiarity
That its time to now again unknow.

# SUNDAY'S IN LOVE

Are there Sunday's in love?
What an amazing piece of question.
"Me space'is the term they use
Or sabbatical is a refined version.
Gaps are created to breathe
Words take a backseat]
Are bonds required to recharge?
Is the new-age relationship based on mirage?
Togetherness is an antonym for them
My silver streaks speak of an era
Where silences filled up the inches between
And Sunday's made the most of the love sheen.

# TAKE ME BACK

Take me back to the sands of time
Where drops of water flows from wine
Horizons are stretched
And coconut trees loom low
Where white fluffy waves touch and go
And beauty lurks in refined gleams
Deep sands beneath the toes
Rhythmic and random colors explode
My soul relaxes on the beachy shore.

# FRAGRANCE

I wore the fragrance this morning
The exquisite perfume of confidence
A love-affair it started
In hopes and dreams
The enchanted smell wafted warm breeze
The waves of drops held me there
The 'Ittr' Ma put on back of her tiny ears
The molecules occupied the space in head
Citrus cologne as my Dad splash
Attire to smell good is easy-peasy
It has to be persona's enduring scent .

# GUILTY

I am guilty of being innocent
Innocent to the questions
Questions which had simple answers
Answers which were rightfully owned
I am guilty of being innocent
For those unspoken answers
As now there will be no peace
I am guilty of being innocent
For the lifelong wait.

# HER BIRTHDAY

And then She came
To the unprepared , flawed us.
We embraced the life again
And silently She smiled.
Space and time became exponential
As grew the graph of her smile.
We made the cocoon , dismantled it
Recreated and smashed again.
And silently She smiled.
The array of emotions were awakened
The circle became small
Glorious glimpses flashed so often
Love became a fact so common
And silently She smiled
The beginnings , new wings and words aplenty
The path criss-cross and mazes a many
She sleeps unfazed tonight
Her tiny slip ons become magical
Her silhouette is aligned to get the potion
As silently they are smiling somewhere
Whispering nothing's and ramblings so many
They are ready today
To embrace the sparkle again
Of year she marks of being a blessing.

# HIBISCUS

The soft wisp of hair left unruly
Slight wave on face that is sleepy
The flower girl walks on the tangent of the leaves
Oh the tiny whispers call her for treat
She waves to the trees on the planet of red
Behind the bunches of hibiscus plaids
Silent eyes speak volumes of love
Which paints the garden of mind plush hue
The calmness in her esteem
Shines and escalates her glow of the soul.
The flower girl sleeps under the sky
Stars pour dew and moon goes shy.

www.ingramcontent.com/pod-product-compliance
Lightning Source LLC
LaVergne TN
LVHW041443170726

843492LV00008B/2786